PREGNANCY COOKBOOK

40+ Tart, Ice-Cream and Pie recipes for a healthy and balanced Pregnancy diet

TABLE OF CONTENTS

Introduction

Pregnancy recipes for personal enjoyment but also for family enjoyment. You will love them for sure for how easy it is to prepare them.

PANCAKES

Serves: *4*

Prep Time: *10* Minutes

Cook Time: *10* Minutes

Total Time: *20* Minutes

INGREDIENTS

- 1 cup millet flour
- ½ cup soy flour
- 1 tablespoon baking powder
- ¼ tsp salt
- 1 egg
- 1 cup water
- 2 tablespoons oil

DIRECTIONS

1. In a bowl mix all dry ingredients
2. Stir together all liquids and add to dry ingredients
3. Bake on griddle for 1-2 minutes per side
4. Remove and serve

BLUEBERRY PANCAKES

Serves: *4*

Prep Time: *10* Minutes

Cook Time: *20* Minutes

Total Time: *30* Minutes

INGREDIENTS

- 1 cup whole wheat flour
- ¼ tsp baking soda
- ¼ tsp baking powder
- 1 cup blueberries
- 2 eggs
- 1 cup milk

DIRECTIONS

1. In a bowl combine all ingredients together and mix well
2. In a skillet heat olive oil
3. Pour ¼ of the batter and cook each pancake for 1-2 minutes per side
4. When ready remove from heat and serve

ALMOND PANCAKES

Serves: *4*
Prep Time: *10* Minutes

Cook Time: *30* Minutes

Total Time: *40* Minutes

INGREDIENTS

- **1 cup whole wheat flour**
- **¼ tsp baking soda**
- **¼ tsp baking powder**
- **1 cup almonds**
- **2 eggs**
- **1 cup milk**

DIRECTIONS

1. **In a bowl combine all ingredients together and mix well**
2. **In a skillet heat olive oil**
3. **Pour ¼ of the batter and cook each pancake for 1-2 minutes per side**
4. **When ready remove from heat and serve**

BANANA PANCAKES

Serves: ***4***
Prep Time: ***10*** Minutes

Cook Time: ***20*** Minutes

Total Time: ***30*** Minutes

INGREDIENTS

- 1 cup whole wheat flour
- ¼ tsp baking soda
- ¼ tsp baking powder
- 1 cup mashed banana
- 2 eggs
- 1 cup milk

DIRECTIONS

1. **In a bowl combine all ingredients together and mix well**
2. **In a skillet heat olive oil**
3. **Pour ¼ of the batter and cook each pancake for 1-2 minutes per side**
4. **When ready remove from heat and serve**

STRAWBERRY PANCAKES

Serves: *4*

Prep Time: *10* Minutes

Cook Time: *20* Minutes

Total Time: *30* Minutes

INGREDIENTS

- 1 cup whole wheat flour
- ¼ tsp baking soda
- ¼ tsp baking powder
- 1 cup strawberries
- 2 eggs
- 1 cup milk

DIRECTIONS

1. In a bowl combine all ingredients together and mix well
2. In a skillet heat olive oil
3. Pour ¼ of the batter and cook each pancake for 1-2 minutes per side
4. When ready remove from heat and serve

SIMPLE PANCAKES

Serves: *4*
Prep Time: *10* Minutes

Cook Time: *30* Minutes

Total Time: *40* Minutes

INGREDIENTS

- **1 cup whole wheat flour**
- **¼ tsp baking soda**
- **¼ tsp baking powder**
- **2 eggs**
- **1 cup milk**

DIRECTIONS

1. **In a bowl combine all ingredients together and mix well**
2. **In a skillet heat olive oil**
3. **Pour ¼ of the batter and cook each pancake for 1-2 minutes per side**
4. **When ready remove from heat and serve**

GINGERBREAD MUFFINS

Serves: *8-12*

Prep Time: ***10*** Minutes

Cook Time: ***20*** Minutes

Total Time: ***30*** Minutes

INGREDIENTS

- **2 eggs**
- **1 tablespoon olive oil**
- **1 cup milk**
- **2 cups whole wheat flour**
- **1 tsp baking soda**
- **¼ tsp baking soda**
- **1 tsp ginger**
- **1 tsp cinnamon**
- **¼ cup molasses**

DIRECTIONS

1. **In a bowl combine all dry ingredients**
2. **In another bowl combine all dry ingredients**
3. **Combine wet and dry ingredients together**
4. **Fold in ginger and mix well**
5. **Pour mixture into 8-12 prepared muffin cups, fill 2/3 of the cups**

6. **Bake for 18-20 minutes at 375 F**
7. **When ready remove from the oven and serve**

BANANA MUFFINS

Serves: *8-12*

Prep Time: ***10*** Minutes

Cook Time: ***20*** Minutes

Total Time: ***30*** Minutes

INGREDIENTS

- **2 eggs**
- **1 tablespoon olive oil**
- **1 cup milk**
- **2 cups whole wheat flour**
- **1 tsp baking soda**
- **¼ tsp baking soda**
- **1 tsp cinnamon**
- **1 cup mashed banana**

DIRECTIONS

1. **In a bowl combine all dry ingredients**
2. **In another bowl combine all dry ingredients**
3. **Combine wet and dry ingredients together**
4. **Fold in mashed banana and mix well**
5. **Pour mixture into 8-12 prepared muffin cups, fill 2/3 of the cups**
6. **Bake for 18-20 minutes at 375 F**

7. **When ready remove from the oven and serve**

BLUEBERRY MUFFINS

Serves: *8-12*

Prep Time: ***10*** Minutes

Cook Time: ***20*** Minutes

Total Time: ***30*** Minutes

INGREDIENTS

- **2 eggs**
- **1 tablespoon olive oil**
- **1 cup milk**
- **2 cups whole wheat flour**
- **1 tsp baking soda**
- **¼ tsp baking soda**
- **1 tsp cinnamon**
- **1 cup blueberries**

DIRECTIONS

1. **In a bowl combine all dry ingredients**
2. **In another bowl combine all dry ingredients**
3. **Combine wet and dry ingredients together**
4. **Fold in blueberries and mix well**
5. **Pour mixture into 8-12 prepared muffin cups, fill 2/3 of the cups**
6. **Bake for 18-20 minutes at 375 F**

7. **When ready remove from the oven and serve**

STRAWBERRY MUFFINS

Serves: *8-12*
Prep Time: ***10*** Minutes

Cook Time: ***20*** Minutes

Total Time: ***30*** Minutes

INGREDIENTS

- **2 eggs**
- **1 tablespoon olive oil**
- **1 cup milk**
- **2 cups whole wheat flour**
- **1 tsp baking soda**
- **¼ tsp baking soda**
- **1 tsp cinnamon**
- **1 cup strawberries**

DIRECTIONS

1. **In a bowl combine all dry ingredients**
2. **In another bowl combine all dry ingredients**
3. **Combine wet and dry ingredients together**
4. **Fold in strawberries and mix well**
5. **Pour mixture into 8-12 prepared muffin cups, fill 2/3 of the cups**
6. **Bake for 18-20 minutes at 375 F**

7. **When ready remove from the oven and serve**

CHOCOLATE MUFFINS

Serves: *8-12*

Prep Time: ***10*** Minutes

Cook Time: ***20*** Minutes

Total Time: ***30*** Minutes

INGREDIENTS

- **2 eggs**
- **1 tablespoon olive oil**
- **1 cup milk**
- **2 cups whole wheat flour**
- **1 tsp baking soda**
- **¼ tsp baking soda**
- **1 tsp cinnamon**
- **1 cup chocolate chips**

DIRECTIONS

1. **In a bowl combine all dry ingredients**
2. **In another bowl combine all dry ingredients**
3. **Combine wet and dry ingredients together**
4. **Fold in chocolate chips and mix well**
5. **Pour mixture into 8-12 prepared muffin cups, fill 2/3 of the cups**
6. **Bake for 18-20 minutes at 375 F**

7. **When ready remove from the oven and serve**

SIMPLE MUFFINS

Serves: *8-12*

Prep Time: ***10*** Minutes

Cook Time: ***20*** Minutes

Total Time: ***30*** Minutes

INGREDIENTS

- 2 eggs
- 1 tablespoon olive oil
- 1 cup milk
- 2 cups whole wheat flour
- 1 tsp baking soda
- ¼ tsp baking soda
- 1 tsp cinnamon

DIRECTIONS

1. In a bowl combine all dry ingredients
2. In another bowl combine all dry ingredients
3. Combine wet and dry ingredients together
4. Pour mixture into 8-12 prepared muffin cups, fill 2/3 of the cups
5. Bake for 18-20 minutes at 375 F
6. When ready remove from the oven and serve

BERRY FRENCH TOAST

Serves: 2
Prep Time: *10* Minutes

Cook Time: *15* Minutes

Total Time: *25* Minutes

INGREDIENTS

- **2 bread slices**
- **1tsp lemon juice**
- **1 tsp vanilla extract**
- **2 eggs**
- **¼ cup heavy cream**
- **1 tsp cinnamon**
- **¼ cup maple syrup**
- **1 cup blueberries**

DIRECTIONS

1. **In a bowl combine all ingredients for the dipping**
2. **Dip the bread slices in the mixture and let them soak for 2-3 minutes**
3. **When ready fry the bread for 2-3 minutes per side**
4. **When ready remove from the skillet and serve with blueberries and maple syrup**

POHA WAFFLES

Serves: ***4***

Prep Time: ***10*** Minutes

Cook Time: ***10*** Minutes

Total Time: ***20*** Minutes

INGREDIENTS

- **½ cup rice flour**
- **1 tsp baking soda**
- **1 banana**
- **½ tsp salt**
- **2 tablespoons oil**
- **½ cup milk**
- **1 tsp cider vinegar**
- **1 egg**
- **½ cup quinoa flakes**
- **1 tablespoon honey**

DIRECTIONS

1. **In a bowl mix all dry ingredients**
2. **Separate egg yolk from egg white and beet egg white**
3. **Mix egg yolk with milk, honey, wet fruit and add dry ingredients to mixture**
4. **Add cider vinegar and mix gently**

5. **Pour mixture into waffle iron**
6. **When remove and serve**

BREAKFAST BISCUITS

Serves: *12*
Prep Time: *10* Minutes

Cook Time: *15* Minutes

Total Time: *25* Minutes

INGREDIENTS

- **2 cups flour**
- **1 tsp xantham gum**
- **½ tsp salt**
- **4 tablespoons margarine**
- **¾ cup vance's darifree**
- **1 tablespoon baking powder**
- **1 tsp sugar**

DIRECTIONS

1. **Preheat oven to 425 F**
2. **Toss together all ingredients, gather into a ball**
3. **Form small biscuits and bake for 12-15 minutes**
4. **Remove and serve**

INDIAN PANCAKES

Serves: 2

Prep Time: *10* Minutes

Cook Time: *10* Minutes

Total Time: *20* Minutes

INGREDIENTS

- 1 cup chick pea flour
- 1 tablespoon ginger
- 1/3 cup chopped green onions
- 1 cu water

DIRECTIONS

1. **In a bowl whisk all ingredients together**
2. **Pour mixture in a pan and cook 1-2 minutes per side**
3. **Remove and serve with honey**

COOKED MILLET

Serves: *4*
Prep Time: *10* Minutes

Cook Time: *20* Minutes

Total Time: *30* Minutes

INGREDIENTS

- 1 cup millet grains
- 3 cups water

DIRECTIONS

1. **In a pot toast 1 cup of millet grains until golden brown**
2. **Add water and bring to boil, stir constantly**
3. **Cook on low heat for 20 minutes**
4. **Remove and serve**

MUFFIN MIX

Serves: ***10***

Prep Time: ***10*** Minutes

Cook Time: ***20*** Minutes

Total Time: ***30*** Minutes

INGREDIENTS

- **¼ cup sugar**
- **¼ tsp salt**
- **¼ tsp vanilla**
- **2 tablespoons shortening**
- **1 tablespoon baking powder**
- **½ cup milk**
- **2 eggs**
- **1 cup GF flour mix**

DIRECTIONS

1. **In a bowl mix together shortening with sugar**
2. **Sift together the flour, milk, baking powder, salt and beaten eggs**
3. **Stir in vanilla and pour muffin mixture into muffin cups**
4. **Bake at 325 F for 15-20 minutes**
5. **Remove and serve**

BANANA BREAD

Serves: *4*

Prep Time: *10* Minutes

Cook Time: *60* Minutes

Total Time: *70* Minutes

INGREDIENTS

- **1 cup soy flour**
- **1 ½ tsp baking powder**
- **½ tsp xanthan gum**
- **½ tsp salt**
- **½ cup mashed banana**
- **2/4 tsp baking soda**
- **½ cup shortening**
- **½ cup potato starch flour**
- **½ cup rice flour**
- **2/3 up honey**
- **2 eggs beaten**

DIRECTIONS

1. **In a bowl mix all dry ingredients together**
2. **Mix honey and shortening until light and fluffy and add beaten eggs**

3. **Add dry ingredients with the mashed banana and mix until smooth**
4. **Pour mixture into a loaf pan and bake for 60 minutes at 325 F**

FRITTER

Serves: *4*

Prep Time: *10* Minutes

Cook Time: *20* Minutes

Total Time: *30* Minutes

INGREDIENTS

- **2 cornstarch**
- **2 tablespoons rice flour**
- **2 packs rise yeast**
- **1 egg**
- **cornstarch bread**
- **5 tablespoons potato starch**
- **2 tablespoons almonds**
- **2 cups water**
- **2 tablespoons oil**
- **1 tsp salt**
- **¼ cup sugar**
- **1 tsp xanthan gum**

DIRECTIONS

1. **In a bowl combine all dry ingredients**
2. **Add hot water to mixture and beat with a mixer for 4-5 minutes**

3. **Add oil and beat again for 2-3 minutes**
4. **Cook until golden brown, remove and serve**

HOT CHOCOLATE MIX

Serves: ***4***

Prep Time: ***10*** Minutes

Cook Time: ***30*** Minutes

Total Time: ***40*** Minutes

INGREDIENTS

- **4 cups dari-free**
- **1 cup sugar**
- **¼ tsp salt**
- **¾ cup cocoa powder**

DIRECTIONS

1. **In a bowl mix all ingredients**
2. **Place 4 tablespoons mix in a cup**
3. **Add boiling water and stir to dissolve mix**

PANCAKE SYRUP

Serves: ***4***

Prep Time: ***10*** Minutes

Cook Time: ***30*** Minutes

Total Time: ***40*** Minutes

INGREDIENTS

- **3 cups corn syrup**
- **1 cup maple syrup**

DIRECTIONS

1. **In a jar mix maple syrup with corn syrup**
2. **100% pure ingredients are required for this GFCF recipe**

PINEAPPLE BREAKFAST CAKE

Serves: ***4***

Prep Time: ***10*** Minutes

Cook Time: ***40*** Minutes

Total Time: ***50*** Minutes

INGREDIENTS

- **3 eggs**
- **1 tablespoon cinnamon**
- **18-ounce can pineapple**
- **1 tsp baking soda**
- **1 tsp GF vanilla**
- **4 ounces GF bread**
- **½ cup sugar**

DIRECTIONS

1. **In a blender add crushed pineapple and the rest of the ingredients, blend until smooth**
2. **Pour mixture into a pan and sprinkle with cinnamon**
3. **Bake at 325 F for 40 minutes**

SCRAMBLED EGGS WITH RICE

Serves: ***4***

Prep Time: ***10*** Minutes

Cook Time: ***10*** Minutes

Total Time: ***20*** Minutes

INGREDIENTS

- ¼ cup onion
- ¼ cup margarine
- 4 eggs
- 1/3 cup rice
- ½ tsp salt
- 1 cup grated cheese

DIRECTIONS

1. **In a pot cook margarine and onion until golden brown**
2. **In a bowl mix milk and eggs, add rice, cheese and salt**
3. **Pour mixture over onion and cook or 4-5 minutes**
4. **Remove and serve**

TART RECIPES

APPLE TART

Serves: *6-8*

Prep Time: 25 Minutes

Cook Time: 25 Minutes

Total Time: *50* Minutes

INGREDIENTS

- pastry sheets

FILLING

- 1 tsp lemon juice
- 3 oz. brown sugar
- 1 lb. apples
- 150 ml double cream
- 2 eggs

DIRECTIONS

1. Preheat oven to 400 F, unfold pastry sheets and place them on a baking sheet
2. Toss together all ingredients together and mix well
3. Spread mixture in a single layer on the pastry sheets
4. Before baking decorate with your desired fruits
5. Bake at 400 F for 22-25 minutes or until golden brown

6. **When ready remove from the oven and serve**

CHOCHOLATE TART

Serves: *6-8*

Prep Time: *25* Minutes

Cook Time: *25* Minutes

Total Time: *50* Minutes

INGREDIENTS

- pastry sheets
- 1 tsp vanilla extract
- ½ lb. caramel
- ½ lb. black chocolate
- 4-5 tablespoons butter
- 3 eggs
- ¼ lb. brown sugar

DIRECTIONS

1. Preheat oven to 400 F, unfold pastry sheets and place them on a baking sheet
2. Toss together all ingredients together and mix well
3. Spread mixture in a single layer on the pastry sheets
4. Before baking decorate with your desired fruits
5. Bake at 400 F for 22-25 minutes or until golden brown
6. When ready remove from the oven and serve

PEACH PECAN PIE

Serves: *8-12*

Prep Time: *15* Minutes

Cook Time: *35* Minutes

Total Time: *50* Minutes

INGREDIENTS

- **4-5 cups peaches**
- **1 tablespoon preserves**
- **1 cup sugar**
- **4 small egg yolks**
- **¼ cup flour**
- **1 tsp vanilla extract**

DIRECTIONS

1. **Line a pie plate or pie form with pastry and cover the edges of the plate depending on your preference**
2. **In a bowl combine all pie ingredients together and mix well**
3. **Pour the mixture over the pastry**
4. **Bake at 400-425 F for 25-30 minutes or until golden brown**
5. **When ready remove from the oven and let it rest for 15 minutes**

BLUEBERRY PIE

Serves: *8-12*
Prep Time: *15* Minutes

Cook Time: *35* Minutes

Total Time: *50* Minutes

INGREDIENTS

- pastry sheets
- ¼ tsp lavender
- 1 cup brown sugar
- 4-5 cups blueberries
- 1 tablespoon lemon juice
- 1 cup almonds
- 2 tablespoons butter

DIRECTIONS

1. Line a pie plate or pie form with pastry and cover the edges of the plate depending on your preference
2. In a bowl combine all pie ingredients together and mix well
3. Pour the mixture over the pastry
4. Bake at 400-425 F for 25-30 minutes or until golden brown
5. When ready remove from the oven and let it rest for 15 minutes

PUMPKIN PIE

Serves: *8-12*

Prep Time: *15* Minutes

Cook Time: *35* Minutes

Total Time: *50* Minutes

INGREDIENTS

- pastry sheets
- 1 cup buttermilk
- 1 can pumpkin
- 1 cup sugar
- 1 tsp cinnamon
- 1 tsp vanilla extract
- 2 eggs

DIRECTIONS

1. Line a pie plate or pie form with pastry and cover the edges of the plate depending on your preference
2. In a bowl combine all pie ingredients together and mix well
3. Pour the mixture over the pastry
4. Bake at 400-425 F for 25-30 minutes or until golden brown
5. When ready remove from the oven and let it rest for 15 minutes

SMOOTHIE RECIPES

GREEN SMOOTHIE

Serves: *1*

Prep Time: *5* Minutes

Cook Time: *5* Minutes

Total Time: *10* Minutes

INGREDIENTS

- **1 banana**
- **1 cup pineapple chunks**
- **1 cup mango chunks**
- **1 cup kale**
- **1 cup ice**
- **½ cup almond milk**

DIRECTIONS

1. **In a blender place all ingredients and blend until smooth**
2. **Pour smoothie in a glass and serve**

WAKE UP SMOOTHIE

Serves: *1*

Prep Time: *5* Minutes

Cook Time: *5* Minutes

Total Time: ***10*** Minutes

INGREDIENTS

- **1 banana**
- **1 cup coffee**
- **¼ cup milk**
- **1 pinch cinnamon**
-

DIRECTIONS

1. **In a blender place all ingredients and blend until smooth**
2. **Pour smoothie in a glass and serve**

RASPBERRY SMOOTHIE

Serves: *1*

Prep Time: *5* Minutes

Cook Time: *5* Minutes

Total Time: ***10*** Minutes

INGREDIENTS

- **1 cup raspberries**
- **½ cup coconut milk**
- **1 cup mango**
- **¼ cup pear juice**

DIRECTIONS

1. **In a blender place all ingredients and blend until smooth**
2. **Pour smoothie in a glass and serve**

CHOCOLATE SMOOTHIE

Serves: *1*
Prep Time: *5* Minutes

Cook Time: *5* Minutes

Total Time: ***10*** Minutes

INGREDIENTS

- 1 banana
- 1 tsp cocoa powder
- 1 cup almond milk
- 1 cup chocolate chips

DIRECTIONS

1. **In a blender place all ingredients and blend until smooth**
2. **Pour smoothie in a glass and serve**

PROTEIN SMOOTHIE

Serves: *1*
Prep Time: *5* Minutes

Cook Time: *5* Minutes

Total Time: *10* Minutes

INGREDIENTS

- **¼ avocado**
- **¼ cup Greek Yogurt**
- **1 tablespoon honey**
- **1 cup low-fat milk**
- **1 cup ice**
- **¼ cup spinach**

DIRECTIONS

1. **In a blender place all ingredients and blend until smooth**
2. **Pour smoothie in a glass and serve**

SUNSHINE SMOOTHIE

Serves: *1*
Prep Time: *5* Minutes

Cook Time: *5* Minutes

Total Time: ***10*** Minutes

INGREDIENTS

- **1 banana**
- **1 cup almond milk**
- **Juice from 1 orange**
- **1 tablespoon goji berries**
- **1 cup ice**

DIRECTIONS

1. **In a blender place all ingredients and blend until smooth**
2. **Pour smoothie in a glass and serve**

MANGO SMOOTHIE

Serves:	*1*	
Prep Time:	*5*	Minutes
Cook Time:	*5*	Minutes
Total Time:	***10***	Minutes

INGREDIENTS

- **1 cup mango**
- **1 cup spinach**
- **¼ avocado**
- **1 cup milk**
- **1 tsp vanilla extract**

DIRECTIONS

1. **In a blender place all ingredients and blend until smooth**
2. **Pour smoothie in a glass and serve**

PEACH SMOOTHIE

Serves: *1*
Prep Time: *5* Minutes

Cook Time: *5* Minutes

Total Time: *10* Minutes

INGREDIENTS

- **1 cup almond milk**
- **2 peaches**
- **1 banana**
- **1 cup ice**
- **1 tablespoon honey**
- **1 tsp almond extract**

DIRECTIONS

1. **In a blender place all ingredients and blend until smooth**
2. **Pour smoothie in a glass and serve**

PUMPKIN SMOOTHIE

Serves: *1*
Prep Time: *5* Minutes

Cook Time: *5* Minutes

Total Time: *10* Minutes

INGREDIENTS

- **¼ cup oats**
- **½ cup puree**
- **4 oz. Greek Yogurt**
- **1 apple**
- **½ cup almond milk**
- **1 cup ice**

DIRECTIONS

1. **In a blender place all ingredients and blend until smooth**
2. **Pour smoothie in a glass and serve**

COFFE ICE-CREAM

Serves: *6-8*

Prep Time: *15* Minutes

Cook Time: *15* Minutes

Total Time: *30* Minutes

INGREDIENTS

- **4 egg yolks**
- **1 cup black coffee**
- **2 cups heavy cream**
- **1 cup half-and-half**
- **1 cup brown sugar**
- **1 tsp vanilla extract**

DIRECTIONS

1. **In a saucepan whisk together all ingredients**
2. **Mix until bubbly**
3. **Strain into a bowl and cool**
4. **Whisk in favorite fruits and mix well**
5. **Cover and refrigerate for 2-3 hours**
6. **Pour mixture in the ice-cream maker and follow manufacturer instructions**

STRAWBERRY ICE-CREAM

Serves: *6-8*

Prep Time: *15* Minutes

Cook Time: *15* Minutes

Total Time: *30* Minutes

INGREDIENTS

- **1 lb. strawberries**
- **½ cup sugar**
- **1 tablespoon vanilla extract**
- **1 cup heavy cram**
- **1-pint vanilla**

DIRECTIONS

1. **In a saucepan whisk together all ingredients**
2. **Mix until bubbly**
3. **Strain into a bowl and cool**
4. **Whisk in favorite fruits and mix well**
5. **Cover and refrigerate for 2-3 hours**
6. **Pour mixture in the ice-cream maker and follow manufacturer instructions**
7. **Serve when ready**

THANK YOU FOR READING THIS BOOK!

CPSIA information can be obtained
at www.ICGtesting.com
Printed in the USA
BVHW030639250321
603406BV00001B/66